Nevertheless

Nevertheless
©2025 Joanne Hayhurst

Published by *Hobo Jungle Press*
St. Vincent & the Grenadines, W.I.
Sharon, Connecticut, USA

First edition
April 2025
Printed in the United States of America
ISBN #979-8-9922251-4-3
Library of Congress Control #2025936290

Nevertheless

Poetry by
Joanne Hayhurst

This collection of poems
is dedicated to long marriage

Contents

The Expulsion

In another version, he remains.
She's made to take the serpent. The gate's bolted

behind them. Her mind is a sprung trap snapped
shut. In that reverberating echo,

cold metal in a shaking of no air, they are
driven out, abandoned. She drags herself

through panic's trap, past thought or question,
she moves

into the north where conifers darken
deep ravines. Although no word is spoken—

hours, days, a year? how many moltings?
the reviled grow to know another language

as they move behind the line of memory.
She learns reptilian dry and silent ways,

his long chain of vertebrae, his smooth
armor of scales. As though they shared a common

metal, they're drawn toward the pole. North
and north, the snake begins to sicken, slow,

brought below a temperature of zero.
She stumbles, falls, crawls the last mountain pass

to a cave within a wall of pines,
protected from the howling wind

where she can warm them, make a fire.
She brings a fierce and focused stillness

into the dank air, stirs the kindling,
blows a budding spark, the fire blooms.

My Seasons, a Breakdown

summer

> I didn't finish the book begun in Ireland—
> it didn't seem to matter how it ended, and I didn't
> take much pleasure from the garden. Rushing,
> I'd snip quickly, fill a vase, stick it in the kitchen,
> but the damn things kept dying, turning clear
> water to slime. I didn't get around to lying
> in the hammock in the shade of apple trees,
> and I didn't say goodbye, but I drank gin and plenty
> of it, and saw my mother for an hour every day.

fall

> I didn't finish two books for book club
> and I forgot the plot of number three. I didn't
> carve our pumpkin Halloween. I didn't hike
> when leaves had stormed the hills again with color,
> and I didn't say goodbye, although I should have
> years ago, but I drank Pinot Noir and Chardonnay,
> and every Sunday cooked a supper for my mother.

winter

> I'll get through Christmas, somehow do the shopping
> and read that book of poems I've set aside.
> I'll decorate the house with boughs and branches,
> make a fire every night and sip green tea.
> I'll say goodbye at last because I have to,
> and my mother? If she's still alive?
> I'll figure something out.

spring

> I can't imagine spring.

The Procedure

Let's just get it done:
insert your instrument,
snake it up and through me.
I'll consider windows

take my mind away
to fix it far—beyond
your probe, out there to where,
far off—past building bricks,

a parking lot, a hill—
I see, or maybe I
imagine, two properties
defined by one stone wall.

I'm thinking how they made it
without cement, held fast
by lodge of stone on stone;
how it heaves and settles,

mouths the earth's slow movements,
how it moans. Meantime, you find
your way through dark, as water
finds a trail between

two stones, and prowls around
until it slows with winter,
freezes and expands,
prying loose the parts.

I wonder, though, what
it takes to touch the hearting,
the center of the wall,
its stony strength—

what it takes to wreck it.

Knossos

Beyond the groves of olives plucked, pressed
to gleaming oils and grapevines barely budding,
past village trees of swollen lemons jeweling green,
I stand before the frescoes and behold,
as if they were immortal or imagined,
clay-deep reds, clear blues, swimming dolphins,
dancers, acrobats bull-leaping.
So I think of you and me, what we seized
of grace and joy and whimsy—
peacock-feather proud, you were
my Prince of Lilies. We imagined years,
gorgeous as two frescoed griffins,
but deep under us, as they must,
earth's tectonic plates were moaning.

Meteor Shower: November, 4 a.m.

Barefoot, we stood on the deck's wide planks,
glazed with an icy dew, but didn't complain,
the way you wouldn't say a cathedral is cold
though you shiver.

Silent, we stood at the bottom of night.
"There," I pointed and whispered, "the dipper,"
as if I'd explained when the fires had died.
Single cinders of star slipped,
slid down the night, another and more.
How to hold on to a beautiful thing?

How many mornings in twenty-three years
have you wakened me with the trace, as of light,
of your fingers at my thigh, that eloquence of silence
that tells where we are, not why.

A.A. Meeting: First Time

It's 5 p.m., our cocktail hour

What he says:

It's late; it's Sunday afternoon.
Where are you going? Why?

What she doesn't say:

If time on earth were mountain
and my daily life were dance,
I could say I've been waltzing
along ridges, that I've known
an indifferent sure wind
has been easing me toward
this precipice, this cliff.
As my slow dance turns
to tarantella, my steps
to slippery chance
I see bottom.

Bridal Shower

The table's been arranged for fantasy:
White lacy cloth, a crystal vase of flowers
In seven shades of blush. The bride-to-be's
Demure. Next to her, ribboned gifts tower,
Pink boxes for a dowry. Nothing's changed.
She oohs and we sip doll-sized cups filled
With pastel punch. Each ladle tips a chain
Of violets locked in ice. I'm offered well-chilled
Strawberries. How to eat them properly?
Too red, they're bigger than a husband's thumb;
The tip that's sweet with chocolate, I can see
Will crack off, stain my ironed blouse, like some
Words I spilt last night that spoiled dreams.
To lose your name's exactly what it seems.

Mute Swans

Late afternoon of the day before time collapses,
succumbs to unstoppable dark (for tomorrow
night will drop early; we'll light a lamp, make soup
bled from marrow) we've stolen an hour,
gone down through woods to the water. Cold
ankles, cold shins, we right the canoe, shove
off into the stillness to paddle shadows of pine,
blood-orange leaves, the ropy reflections of birch-bone.
The sun's sinking fast when in the last light we spot them,
gliding like royalty drawn on a barge, feral
descendants of birds that grew fat and content
on formal waters. And now an arced white wing,
raised scapular, a nod? some silent signal
as we come near. A long-necked unfolding: they rise,
synchronized, draw breath, release one vowel,
the keening you hear in your head when you waken in fear.
They're forming a circle, the terrible singing is closing
its ring, we're trapped inside what has been circumscribed,
the life we've chosen now chokes us. I turn to see
you're holding your paddle like a weapon;
                                   your eyes are on me.

Clean

Not the wet white
of bleached bedsheets,
that smack
that says
there's some order in this day,
a wind direction
and a drying sun.

More the nothing
between me and me,
as if I'd carved off cartilage
with care, leaving
bone on bone
that scrape
that says
beware.

The Blue Woman

Seven years I worked in a bank that lacked windows, weather, shadow.
Soundproofing wicked at my soul while a screen hummed indifference.

But one midmorning from somewhere I heard a sound,
neither tap-tap nor whirring, it was, instead, a single thin

tinkle, another, a melody played on keys of a toy piano,
tinny and small, but enough to make my heart hurt, to know

I wanted more. I willed the song larger, filled it with daydream:
a garden, full summer, a fruit-bearing, beautiful tree, as music

enlarged past containment. That's when I knew
I'd walk out the door, blank as a sheet freed for scoring.

Persephone in the North

1.

The way they tell it in the Adirondacks,
the lake was smooth as glass; the girl was guiding
her canoe in for the night when brilliance cracked
the sky: a strand of perfect setting
suns lay in flames on water; her urgent
gaze became their dazzled mirror. A stillness
deepened in which, serpent-swift, a cormorant
slid by—graceful, grim—dove, rose,
shook his wings, flung broken suns to glittered
air: spray gilded an inner arm, one breast.
She turned. The sky went wild-eyed, went blind,
bled vision into water. Some say they felt
earth stumble, some say they smelt narcissus.
We only know the dark collapsed around us.

2.

We only know the dark collapsed around us,
time slowed to the muffled tick of falling snow
while below, the girl searched silence
for a friend, reminded of the bone
cold of a rink, as though she'd been left behind
under a metal sky, the buzzer calmed,
clock darkened, in an absence of gloved
clapping, wool blanketing her mind
when, was it a dream? a vision? the tree appeared.
Her withered appetite awoke; one fruit split wide,
released its golden fragrance. She ate
wet crimson flesh, seeds buried deep inside.
Flushed, she saw, in that forbidden dawn,
Hades, patient, waiting, in his hands her crown.

3.

Hades, patient, waiting, in his hands her crown.
A whisper: "Persephone", syllables
like snow slipping into water as his breath
enfolds them both within the nimbus of a kiss.
Enthroned, they reign, thigh by thigh,
yearning muscle, burning skin, grinning
helplessly as two lovers with a secret, while
she settles into dark, some rooted thing.
Above her, drifts of frozen snow grow
dirty, caked and cracked in cellar windows,
while waterfalls, arrested in mid-flow,
hang like tongues torn from mouths mid-sentence,
gossip-stopped: *another girl gone bad...*
think she'll come back to town with April mud?

4.

Think she'll come back to town with April mud?
She turns from him, from sin, from pleasure,
from the darker, older law she'd served.
She rises, gropes her way along a corridor
to a portal's scrape of tangled briars,
glimpses birch in sunlight, sniffs forgotten air,
crosses over. The plow's turned up deep layers:
fertile, fragrant earth; a field opens before her:
the radiant ache of stunning sun, tender
greenery. Beyond the vetch and clover flows
a sea of dandelions that stains her
wet hem yellow as she goes seeking those
who will unfold the rose, expose the wild
center welling from Lake Tear of the Cloud.

5.

The center's welling from Lake Tear of the Cloud
where waters gather, pool, shiver over
moss and stone. The girl, drawn or guided
by an affinity she cannot name, more,
she thinks, like song, climbs higher toward the source.
In dark she follows river sound: the weaving
rush of weeping stone and watered stars
and finds, at last, wet midnight, black and brimming,
gazes deep into the sky-reflecting pool,
cups water in her hands, drinks constellations,
understands. It is she who will
set free the rose, release the scented seasons,
quick! before the cold and common story's back,
the way they tell it in the Adirondacks.

Sixty-eight Days Sober,
on the Beach in Mexico

Our long-absent friends arrive—
greetings continue beyond the time
I can get a taxi to
the AA English-speaking meeting;
I swallow back panic, but
it rises, thickening as we stand
in sand and laugh, catching up.
Is it a slight shift in stance
that signals us to check around?
There, the beach-side bar.

If we do what we used to—
when we were newly coupled, giddy
with our possibilities, before
our babies became children, before
our kids were grown, gone, before
9/11 and betrayals—
we'll head over, order drinks,
another round, a third, laugh
at what a tab we're running up.

One of us (well, me of course)
suggests, instead, we walk along
the shore of where we are, our shadows
lengthen; *tarde* sinks
to *noche*; panic thins as
the first hour passes. I'm halfway
through the next. We're at the bar:
groups of laughy chit chat, stainless
steel cocktail shaker shake/
shake margaritas; the bartender
salts the rims of perfect glasses,
pours four.

Returning

there comes again that embrace
as if hemispheres had not split us

our furies had not blistered my flesh
your anchor had not almost drowned me

and I think I may believe I can want again
your body our heat my body the moment

passes

Retreat

Because my voice is soft, because it's female
and I can't be heard in groups where there's a free-flow
without, oh, so much effort
I've come to love order:
  Robert's Rules
  The format of AA
  Quaker Meetings
  Poetry, and how the seasons rhyme.
Because big voices at big tables erupt
and interrupt, I drowned them out with Pinot
and my smart remarks, forgotten
the next day. This is why
  in a forest that remains in Massachusetts
  in a building that was once a Catholic convent
  in a blue, long-windowed room
  I find comfort sitting with a hundred others
emptying my mind.

The Wedding Portrait Turns Thirty

As if too weary to maintain
the audacity of marriage,
we've faded, phantom-like,
having been exposed
to sun in seven bedrooms;
acid's eaten borders, blurred
our dimensions: veil, arm,
roses, hands—nothing is
clear. Yes, we're together still,
set upon a shelf, bleached
of color, edges, heat. But
something can be said
for aging passion, right?
With it comes the graying
of our rage.

Nevertheless

to mark
the years that follow
we'll need a newer photo,
no frame

Ready or Not

In winter's long-armed dark
I've been drowsing for months

when a sudden dazzle of sunlight
rousts me out. I find myself

driving roads of snowmelt to their farm,
walking wet fields to the sunlit shed:

the first grass is rising; new pigs race
and squeal like kids let out for recess.

My granddaughter's chasing chickens—
all is squawk and grunt and green,

so when she cries *Grammy!*
And in her muddy snowpants

and chicken-shit bottomed boots,
jumps up for a hug, I'm ready.

Paradiso

"And then fine fruit will follow on the flower"
(Beatrice to Dante, Canto XXVII: 148-149)

Stepping in between
rows of just-June greens
Bea leads me to the u-pick.

Pigweed high as her mouth—
she wades into the thick wet
and I'm right behind her

pushing weeds aside.
There's mud.
We're on our knees, but

Look! she says, turning to me.
And there they are, berries,
gleaming as if imagined.

To think this red.
To think Bea knows the way
and shows me.

Love Sonnet
(to the photograph I framed 10 years ago)

My son, your pregnant wife in morning light.
Behind you, new-tilled fields: See? All is right.
What did I know of unbroken boots? You gleam
Fine future. Look! At your knees, two lambs lean
Into sweet coming summer. First rows to hoe,
First birth, my Bea, first boulders rising. You tried
Season after season: weather too wet, soil too dry,
Hail storm, debt storm, divorce, please say no,
Tell me it wasn't a lie! Cry
With me.
        I need to give it up, this controlled rhyme—
        You have your broken hearts and dreams

And I have mine.

Peach Tree at their Barn

Its laden bough
                    split
from its trunk
its still-clinging fruit

ripe final July

                    leaking its sweet heat
away

The Day the Dream Died

insistent the cry
the animal ache
across open acres   beyond
hand-weeded rows: beets, kale,
onions unharvested,
sunflowers falling from
their own weight
as if wanting to mix
self and soil.
The calf, roped
to a post, cries...
behind her, gathered hay bales.
The mother, silenced,
is tractored out
beyond the fields
where wetlands begin   the calf-cry
enters me fills me with
her animal empty
still

Aftermath

My farm son: body-slammed—
how hard the work:
weather-beaten skin, dirt-sweated clothes,
slaughter blood, scum beneath
the frozen water trough, pig-stink.

My wife-severed son: boot-kicked
yet stunning the creation:
laden plants, waves of clover,
basil stirred by wind, potato acre.

I watch the weight-gain of his heart
the dimming of his sky-bright mind
drought of laughter,
still-births of resurrection.

I know the lowing of the dying family cow,
the times I heard her calf cry out,
but there's no counting echoes.

February

snow-struck lawn
two trees: leaf-stripped, bone-still
in the air—scent of chilled tin

I can't breathe

I could fill the feeder with remembered summer:
sunflowers
their oil-soaked centers
(that day of August heat when the child cut
five, six, eleven   laid color in my arms,
the last from their family's now-gone farm)

wait

wait

wing flash, flutter, sound
becomes song   becomes beating hearts --
hear them fill the crisping?   A jay
scrapes blue air, now cardinal red
on white, juncos, chicka-dee-dee-dee
delight

light

breathe

Daphne

I enter where I entered before—
a dozen times, maybe more—a rhythm

catches me quickly: a fine push and glide,
muscles contracting, relaxing in time

with my breathing; then, pumping my arms,
holding my spread thighs apart—straining

with effort—I herringbone-climb to the ridge,
where, finally, I can begin. Sweating,

heart pounding, cheeks flushed and tingling,
I watch the blood-orange sun stain the snow.

*

At a place just beyond three iced-over birch
blazing in brilliant low light, I ski

to a threshold of deep-scented pine;
descending, a child again, I pretend to be

a magician, tapping the snow-dust from boughs
as I slide along showered in gold

to where woods become forest.
Needing no tracks, following animal paths,

I come to a loose-slatted bridge, a place
I don't recognize, a vast field of frozen water,

peculiar light ruptured by twigs,
trapped branches, stumps of chewed trees.

In the deepening stillness, dark's sinking
its chill into me. There's a movement

of water under the ice, the smell
of raw earth below, and on the far side

of the frozen flooding, tall shadows, a dense
grove of laurel. Beyond will or wanting,

my eyes blotting up dark's natural light,
I start to cross to the bower.

One ski is sticking, weighed down with clumps
of wet snow. I free it, drag forward,

but heavily. My motions have slowed, grown thicker,
my toes have gone numb. Beyond thought or logic,

images rise of Daphne pursued,
terrorized, bark is climbing her thighs.

I've come close enough, we're sharing
one shadow, when I hear the stirring of leaves

as if she had whispered, breath at my neck,
as if she had shuddered, I shiver too.

*

I slap my thighs, force blood to rise;
I'll not surrender, myth-paralyzed.

I stagger along her long tree line,
a passageway plunged through the black

lung of night; awkwardly, cold to the bone,
I plant one foot in front of the other,

move through the hours, wanting the morning,
wanting the ending to open.

Narcissus

You forced my stalks from watered stone, tricked
me into rising, weak and pale.
There's too much of a reach
to your artificial househeat—
a paperwhite in winter's
all off-kilter
in a kitchen fogged with soup steam.
You need a bit of spring
to get you through?
What about what I need?
I need a hummingbird
to beat its wild breath
into my crazy flowers.
My tiny whites and yellows
are bending me
beneath their airy
weight,
as though I can't support
simple gladness.
It's taking all my juices
just to be.

The Mercy of May in New England

One morning, while walking, a wind
flung from a South done with sorrow,
full now with fragrance, ripening spills
visible pollen suspended in heat,
sexual heat of the new, a sudden season
wakening what one remembers:
strawberry blood at the tongue.

Sweet Spontaneous Worship
(after Thomas Merton)

A simple, chosen task: harvest this day's
abundance. From two small trees,
a hammock between them: apples
apples   apples

In morning wet grass, I crouch to examine
windfalls. I've seen a furred animal,
low to the ground, early evenings, snuffing
and searching, she chews what she finds,

enough for all of us

Reach into the boughs stricken with low rays
of sun, as if God needed to make things
perfectly clear. *Snap. Pluck.*

A neighbor asks, "Isn't it overwhelming?"
"No," I say, and know
I mean to praise this bounty:

Overflow me, fill me with September,
I've been hungry so long,
let me swallow God.

Day 23: The Ten-year-old and I Break the Covid-19 Quarantine

Masked, we're climbing into acres—
leafless trees, so much light. Broad

trails, worn to roots and rocks, braiding
through the forest. We keep 6 ft. between us.

Halfway up the first steep slope,
I'm breathing hard. He runs ahead,

comes back. *You okay Grammy?*
On our return we need to cross

a shallow stream, its waters rippling
noon-sun over stones. The boy

drops to all his length, reaches
down the bank. *Cold!* he shouts

so I know he's tugged down his bandana.
The way a soldier crawls, he edges closer.

Close enough to smell the cool, close
enough to drink. I want to lie right there

beside him, tear off my mask, bring water
to my mouth, share the breath between us.

The End of Daylight Savings Time
November 2020

That particular day there comes a snow
of no passion, fat flakes falling
onto dried grasses, a brief blanketing.

Meantime, we humans escalate
our fury. Mask, no mask, we breathe in
rage, breathe out righteousness.
My tribe, yours. We cannot speak
without spitting. But, strange to say,

we pause
we cast a hundred and fifty million ballots,
even more than that.

Now, in the almost-afterwards, days
of kind weather, of short afternoons
brightened by autumn sun effort,
we can grab some calm,
hang on

This was when we didn't know
what came next
or after that

2020 Thanksgiving

Election fury has collapsed
of its own weight, drawing down
an old dark as we find our way
through late November woods,
where, for so many American
years, there was a tended clearing,
some light.

That is the way it was,
right?

New Year's Eve 2020

I wake to faraway sound
left ear as if underwater
am I awake?
It slows thinking
down, not knowing.

This winter's half-hearted
snow comes dripping again.
Is Covid forever?
The children are grown and away
must stay away

months of no company coming
no one invited, no need
to wonder how half-hearing
would work if it matters
who's saying what

when handing me woolen
wet coats, stomping big boots.
No reason for florist flowers
in vases, whispering fragrance,
their near shouts of purple and yellow.

How would I enter
friends' talk of vacations
when—while who's saying what
and where—am I hearing
Covid and *cancelled?*
sound behind me, below

over there

Shostakovich:
Piano Quintet in G Minor, Op. 57

The violist is frail, pale, perhaps a little sickly.
Her neck is bruised. The bruise extends
from clavicle to jawbone. In the center,
a bull's eye: an open wound
that continues, very slightly, weeping.
Her long hair sometimes hides it,
as does her instrument, and the patterned scarf
that separates blue flesh from polished wood.
And the music? I feel, more than hear it.

Her eyes have closed. The bow's dragged
over strings, sucking out what sounds
like someone sobbing. When did she start
to feel the pain? When did this arrangement start?
Why did she repeat it,
repeat it, the way the world repeats itself;
to move from wanting it to knowing it
to having it do damage?
Her eyes have closed. She leans into her instrument
as you'd lean toward a lover, even though you know
he could destroy you. The scherzo slams

against her neck. Again. Again. Repeats
it. Sixty years ago: Stalin's Russia
punches its big fist, but she's
resisting. Evil's spilling
everywhere. Then I swear I hear Ahkmatova's
"I can," to that one who asked,
"Can you describe this?"

This girl is opening her eyes.
She eases the viola from her neck
as silence fills the room, the way the heart,
stunned, will skip a beat
before it can recall what should come next.

Woman Painting Caryatids
For Marjory Reid

One winter in the middle of what has been
her life, she wonders who will sing
the things which most have mattered, and finds
that she is humming. Paper is put down, and snow
light through a window lays itself on her
floorboards. She stands a moment, barefoot.
The warmth is seeping upward while she waits
as if praying, holding palette, holding brush.
What flows from her flows from her
       into figure, falls, forms the merest suggestion
       of torso. The paper fills up with female:
       Rounded reds. Voluminous yellows. Mounded heat's
       expansion. The musky sweet scent of woman's
       first blood. One wet rose spreading its petals
       to sunlight, baring stigma and stamen. Eve's opening
       mouth.

But the painter's wet
brush has been traded for pencil: at the bottom
of what had been billowing breath, she's made
a steel-gray graphite bar: greasy, cold
as a muzzle—God the Father's Great *No*.

Utterly New Thing

I was walking with Sarah whose hair had begun to come back
as tentative tufts. She'd pointed out roadside hydrangea,

their subtlety of uncolor, visible now that summer-deep greens
were draining and vines that climb fence-post and rail

had faded into themselves. Everything extra seemed in retreat
the way the body will give up fingers and limbs to keep the heart

beating blood to the brain, the way the head will give hair.
But memory is malleable and will, it insists, be altered.

Like those feathered first sprouts of her baby-bird skull,
as if she'd become some new thing.

Her large brown eyes were wary, watching for what
would stalk her, raze her again. But we grow weary of *wary*.

We want the world open once more before us,
the beautiful tug of the brush through tangles.

Legacy

Copied into books of careful cursive,
I leave to you the poems I memorized
               while walking, day on day
for decades, footfalls finding rhythms,
phrases flowing finally into mind
               becoming mine.

May you know the anchors of my soul:
               Emily squeezed small,
Adrienne, Sylvia and Bishop—
               iron sunk in sand.

I offer you my years-tugged tides,
penned letters slanting this way, that:
Annabel Lee, Leda, Prufrock—
               moving waters.

See the breaking free, the sudden rip
Pages without lines, without margins:
Donne, Hopkins, William Carlos Williams—
               battered air

Look beneath the racing current of the known;
here you'll find my own: colors and cross-outs—
               these ink-smeared
                  particulars

Downsizing

From the file drawer
filled with manila folders
holding my poems arranged
alphabetically of course
and each one's
multiple preliminaries
on pages of yellow paper,
I begin. Yellow sheets
shush into the recycle bin,
ready for the shredding
of my rough ideas, outlines,
phrases rearranged. I say
to no one: *My handwriting,*
it was beautiful. Drafts
disappear.
I notice
my simmering sauce from
the kitchen—its drifting
aroma in this room. I say
to no one: *No one cares.*
No one will care. Had I
really thought someone
someday would want
to know my process?
shush

Nevertheless

one wonders what lies dormant
inside the self that's you;
there must be something fervent,
right? waiting to undo
itself and unroll like a long
red ribbon taken from your pony
tail—perhaps the lyrics of a song
that wakens you, or it could be
a poem, with you at its heart
wide awake and whole, not part

Acknowledgments

Grateful acknowledgement to the editors of the following publications, in which the following poems appeared:

Blueline: "Bridal Shower", "Meteor Shower", "Narcissus"

Chaffin Journal: "The Procedure";

The Pinch: "Clean";

Prairie Schooner: "The Expulsion"

Red Cedar Review: "The Blue Woman"

Reed: "Knossos";

River City: "Mute Swans"

Southwest Review: "Persephone in the North";

The Sow's Ear: "My Seasons, a Breakdown";

Talking River: "Shostakovich", "Woman Painting Caryatids";

Tar Wolf Review: "Utterly New Thing".

www.ingramcontent.com/pod-product-compliance
Lightning Source LLC
Chambersburg PA
CBHW051649120626
46551CB00015B/2278